OUR FAMILY COUNCIL JOURNAL

OUR FAMILY COUNCIL JOURNAL

VOLUME _____

_____ TO _____
DATE   DATE

ᛘ⃝
DESERET
BOOK

Salt Lake City, Utah

Book design © Deseret Book Company

© 2016 M. Russell Ballard Trust

All rights reserved. No part of this book may be reproduced in any form or by any means without permission in writing from the publisher, Deseret Book Company, at permissions@deseretbook .com or P. O. Box 30178, Salt Lake City, Utah 84130. This work is not an official publication of The Church of Jesus Christ of Latter-day Saints. The views expressed herein are the responsibility of the author and do not necessarily represent the position of the Church or of Deseret Book Company.

DESERET BOOK is a registered trademark of Deseret Book Company.

Visit us at DeseretBook.com

ISBN 978-1-62972-305-1

Printed in China
Four Colour Print Group, Nansha, China

10   9   8   7   6   5   4   3   2   1

The Family Council Records of

THE _____ **FAMILY**

An Introduction to
FAMILY
COUNCILS

I believe councils are the most effective way to get real results. Councils are the Lord's way—He created all things in the universe through a heavenly council, as mentioned in the holy scripture (see Abraham 4:26; 5:2–3). But the most basic and fundamental—and perhaps the most important—of all councils is the family council.

Family councils have always been needed. They are, in fact, eternal. We belonged to a family council in the premortal existence, when we lived with our heavenly parents as their spirit children.

A family council, when conducted with love and with Christlike attributes, will counter the impact of modern technology that often distracts us from spending quality time with each other and also tends to bring evil right into our homes.

Please remember that family councils are different from family home evening held on Mondays. Home evenings focus primarily on gospel instruction and family activities. Family councils, on the other hand, can be held on any day of the week, and they are primarily a meeting at which parents listen—to each other and to their children.

I believe there are at least four types of family councils:

First, a general family council consisting of the entire family.

Second, an executive family council consisting of a mother and father.

Third, a limited family council consisting of parents and one child.

Fourth, a one-on-one family council consisting of one parent and one child.

In all of these family council settings, electronic devices need to be turned off so everyone can look at and listen to each other. During family councils and at other appropriate times, you may want to have a basket for the electronic devices so when the family gathers, everyone—including Mom and Dad—can deposit his or her phone, tablet, or MP3 player in the basket.

Let me briefly share with you how each of these types of family councils can work.

First, the full family council includes all family members.

The Church pamphlet entitled *Our Family* states, "This council can meet to discuss family problems, work out finances, make plans, support and strengthen [each other], and pray for one another and for the family unit" (*Our Family: A Practical Guide for Building a Gospel-Centered Home* [pamphlet, 1980], 6).

This council should meet at a predesignated time and is normally more formal than any other type of family council. It should start with a prayer, or it may simply be a natural extension of conversations already started in other settings. Please note that a family council may not always have a formal beginning or ending. When parents are prepared and children listen and participate in the discussion, the family council is truly working!

No matter what our particular family situation is, it is critical that we understand the unique circumstances of each family member. Though we may share DNA, there may be situations and circumstances among us that may make us vastly different from each other and that may require the compassionate collaboration of the family council.

For example, all the talking and sharing and loving in the world may not solve a medical problem or an emotional challenge that one or more family members may be facing. At such times, the family council becomes a place of unity, loyalty, and loving support as outside help is enlisted in the search for solutions.

Siblings, especially the older ones, can be powerful mentors to young children if parents will use the family council to enlist their help and support during times of difficulty and duress. In this way, a family is much like a ward. When the bishop involves ward council members, he can solve problems and accomplish a lot of good in ways he never could do without their help. In a similar fashion, parents need to involve all family members in dealing with challenges and adversity. That way, the power of the family council is put to work. When council members feel they are part of a decision, they become supporters, and specific positive results can be accomplished.

Not every family council consists of two parents and children. Everyone can adapt a family council to take advantage of this divine pattern established by our loving Heavenly Father.

Your family council may look very different than our family council looked when we were raising our seven children. Today our family council consists only of Barbara and me, unless we hold an extended family council that includes our adult children, their spouses, and sometimes our grandchildren and great-grandchildren.

From time to time an expanded family council may be helpful.

An expanded family council can be composed of grandparents and adult children who are not living at home. Even if grandparents or adult children live far away, they can participate in family councils via the telephone, Skype, or FaceTime.

You may want to consider holding the general family council on Sunday, which is the first day of the week; families can review the past week and plan for the coming week. This may be exactly what your family needs to help make the Sabbath a delightful experience.

A simple record kept of these more formal family councils can become a precious family history document in the years to come. Additionally, as decisions are made, such a record can be a valuable resource for implementing and following up on those ideas.

The second type of family council is an executive family council that involves only the parents. During this time together, parents can review each child's physical, emotional, and spiritual needs and his or her progress.

The executive family council is also a good time for wives and husbands to talk about their personal relationships with each other. When Elder Harold B. Lee performed our sealing, he taught us a principle that I believe all couples will find helpful. He said, "Never retire without kneeling together, holding hands, and saying your prayers. Such prayers invite Heavenly Father to counsel us by the power of the Spirit."

The third type of family council is a limited family council. Here, both parents spend time with an individual child in a formal or an informal setting. This is an opportunity for a discussion on *making decisions in advance* about such things as what he or she will and will not do in the future. When such decisions are made, he or she may want to record them for future reference if needed. If your son or daughter sees you as a staunch supporter, this council meeting can establish goals and objectives for the future. This is also a time to carefully listen to serious concerns and challenges that a child may have faced with such things as lack of confidence, abuse, bullying, or fear.

The fourth type of family council is a one-on-one family council involving one parent and one child. This type of family council generally just happens. For example, the parent and child can take advantage of informal opportunities while traveling in the car or working around the house. An outing with one child with either father or mother can provide a special spiritual and emotional bonding time. Calendar these in advance so children can anticipate and look forward to a special time alone with Mom or Dad.

There was a time when the walls of our homes provided all the defense we needed against outside intrusions and influences. We locked the doors, we closed the windows, we shut the gates, and we felt safe, secure, and protected in our own little refuge from the outside world.

Those days are now gone. The physical walls, doors, fences, and gates of our homes cannot prevent unseen invasion from the Internet, the Wi-Fi, the mobile phones, the networks. They can penetrate our homes with just a few clicks and keystrokes.

Fortunately, the Lord has provided a way to counter the invasion of negative technology that can distract us from spending quality time with each other. He has done this by providing the council system to strengthen, protect, safeguard, and nurture our most precious relationships. Children desperately need parents willing to listen to them, and the family council can provide a time during which family members can learn to understand and love one another.

Alma taught, "Counsel with the Lord in all thy doings, and

he will direct thee for good" (Alma 37:37). Inviting the Lord to be part of our family council through prayer will improve our relationships with each other. We can, with Heavenly Father and our Savior's help, become more patient, thoughtful, helpful, forgiving, and understanding as we pray for help. With Their help, we can make our homes a little bit of heaven here on earth.

A family council that is patterned after the councils in heaven, filled with Christlike love, and guided by the Lord's Spirit will help us to protect our family from distractions that can steal our precious time together and protect us from the evils of the world.

Combined with prayer, a family council will invite the presence of the Savior, as He promised: "For where two or three are gathered together in my name, there am I in the midst of them" (Matthew 18:20). Inviting the Spirit of the Lord to be part of your family council brings blessings beyond description.

Please remember that a family council held regularly will help us spot family problems early and nip them in the bud; councils will give each family member a feeling of worth and importance; and most of all they will assist us to be more successful and happy in our precious relationships, within the walls of our homes.

Reminders about family councils:

- They are different from family home evenings.
- They can be held any day of the week but should be at a predesignated time.
- These are primarily meetings where parents listen.
- Electronic devices should be turned off.
- Discussion topics could include: family problems, family finances, future plans, approaches for support during times of difficulty.
- Councils should begin with a prayer.
- When expanded families are involved, consider gathering via telephone, Skype, or FaceTime if meeting live is not an option.

Suggestions for using this journal:

- Designate a family member to take notes for the meeting.
- Notes should be a summary of the key discussions.
- Be sure to capture "next steps" to keep track of commitments made or assignments for follow-up.
- Record humorous or sweet moments that you'll want to remember.
- Use additional note pages when discussion or planning requires. Extra lined pages can be found at the back of the journal. Make note of the page numbers for reference.
- Parents may choose to keep track of sensitive items from their executive councils in a separate journal.

FAMILY
COUNCIL
RECORDS

INVITING

the Spirit of the Lord
to be part of your family
council brings blessings
beyond description.

Date: _____

Prayer: _____ Record Keeper: _____

In Attendance: _____

_____

Discussion Topic: _____

Notes: _____

_____

_____

_____

_____

Next Steps: _____

_____

Discussion Topic: _____

Notes: _____

_____

_____

_____

_____

Next Steps: _____

_____

Other things to remember from our time together: _____

_____

_____

Date: _____

Prayer: _____ Record Keeper: _____

In Attendance: _____

_____

Discussion Topic: _____

Notes: _____

_____

_____

_____

_____

Next Steps: _____

_____

Discussion Topic: _____

Notes: _____

_____

_____

_____

_____

Next Steps: _____

_____

Other things to remember from our time together: _____

_____

_____

Date: _____

Prayer: _____ Record Keeper: _____

In Attendance: _____

_____

Discussion Topic: _____

Notes: _____

_____

_____

_____

_____

Next Steps: _____

_____

Discussion Topic: _____

Notes: _____

_____

_____

_____

_____

Next Steps: _____

_____

Other things to remember from our time together: _____

_____

_____

Date: _____

Prayer: _____ Record Keeper: _____

In Attendance: _____

_____

Discussion Topic: _____

Notes: _____

_____

_____

_____

_____

Next Steps: _____

_____

Discussion Topic: _____

Notes: _____

_____

_____

_____

_____

Next Steps: _____

_____

Other things to remember from our time together: _____

_____

_____

Date: _____

Prayer: _____   Record Keeper: _____

In Attendance: _____

_____

Discussion Topic: _____

Notes: _____

_____

_____

_____

_____

Next Steps: _____

_____

Discussion Topic: _____

Notes: _____

_____

_____

_____

_____

Next Steps: _____

_____

Other things to remember from our time together: _____

_____

_____

Date: _____

Prayer: _____   Record Keeper: _____

In Attendance: _____

_____

Discussion Topic: _____

Notes: _____

_____

_____

_____

_____

_____

Next Steps: _____

_____

Discussion Topic: _____

Notes: _____

_____

_____

_____

_____

_____

Next Steps: _____

_____

Other things to remember from our time together: _____

_____

_____

Date: _____

Prayer: _____ Record Keeper: _____

In Attendance: _____

_____

Discussion Topic: _____

Notes: _____

_____

_____

_____

_____

Next Steps: _____

_____

Discussion Topic: _____

Notes: _____

_____

_____

_____

_____

Next Steps: _____

_____

Other things to remember from our time together: _____

_____

_____

Date: _____

Prayer: _____ Record Keeper: _____

In Attendance: _____
_____

Discussion Topic: _____

Notes: _____
_____
_____
_____
_____

Next Steps: _____
_____

Discussion Topic: _____

Notes: _____
_____
_____
_____
_____

Next Steps: _____
_____

Other things to remember from our time together: _____
_____
_____

Children desperately
need parents willing to
LISTEN to them, and the
family council can provide
a time during which
family members can
learn to understand and
love one another.

Date: _____

Prayer: _____   Record Keeper: _____

In Attendance: _____

_____

Discussion Topic: _____

Notes: _____

_____

_____

_____

_____

Next Steps: _____

_____

Discussion Topic: _____

Notes: _____

_____

_____

_____

_____

Next Steps: _____

_____

Other things to remember from our time together: _____

_____

_____

Date: _____

Prayer: _____ Record Keeper: _____

In Attendance: _____

_____

Discussion Topic: _____

Notes: _____

_____

_____

_____

_____

Next Steps: _____

_____

Discussion Topic: _____

Notes: _____

_____

_____

_____

_____

Next Steps: _____

_____

Other things to remember from our time together: _____

_____

_____

Date: _____

Prayer: _____ Record Keeper: _____

In Attendance: _____

_____

Discussion Topic: _____

Notes: _____

_____

_____

_____

_____

Next Steps: _____

_____

Discussion Topic: _____

Notes: _____

_____

_____

_____

_____

Next Steps: _____

_____

Other things to remember from our time together: _____

_____

_____

Date: _____

Prayer: _____   Record Keeper: _____

In Attendance: _____

_____

Discussion Topic: _____

Notes: _____

_____

_____

_____

_____

Next Steps: _____

_____

Discussion Topic: _____

Notes: _____

_____

_____

_____

_____

Next Steps: _____

_____

Other things to remember from our time together: _____

_____

_____

Whenever there are
two or more members
of a family together and a
discussion is going on,
that is a **COUNCIL!**

Date: _____

Prayer: _____ Record Keeper: _____

In Attendance: _____

_____

Discussion Topic: _____

Notes: _____

_____

_____

_____

_____

Next Steps: _____

_____

Discussion Topic: _____

Notes: _____

_____

_____

_____

_____

Next Steps: _____

_____

Other things to remember from our time together: _____

_____

_____

Date: _____

Prayer: _____   Record Keeper: _____

In Attendance: _____
_____

Discussion Topic: _____

Notes: _____
_____
_____
_____
_____

Next Steps: _____
_____

Discussion Topic: _____

Notes: _____
_____
_____
_____
_____

Next Steps: _____
_____

Other things to remember from our time together: _____
_____
_____

Date: _____

Prayer: _____ Record Keeper: _____

In Attendance: _____

_____

Discussion Topic: _____

Notes: _____

_____

_____

_____

_____

Next Steps: _____

_____

Discussion Topic: _____

Notes: _____

_____

_____

_____

_____

Next Steps: _____

_____

Other things to remember from our time together: _____

_____

_____

Date: _____

Prayer: _____ Record Keeper: _____

In Attendance: _____

_____

Discussion Topic: _____

Notes: _____

_____

_____

_____

_____

Next Steps: _____

_____

Discussion Topic: _____

Notes: _____

_____

_____

_____

_____

Next Steps: _____

_____

Other things to remember from our time together: _____

_____

_____

Date: _____

Prayer: _____ Record Keeper: _____

In Attendance: _____

_____

Discussion Topic: _____

Notes: _____

_____

_____

_____

_____

Next Steps: _____

_____

Discussion Topic: _____

Notes: _____

_____

_____

_____

_____

Next Steps: _____

_____

Other things to remember from our time together: _____

_____

_____

Date: _____

Prayer: _____   Record Keeper: _____

In Attendance: _____

_____

Discussion Topic: _____

Notes: _____

_____

_____

_____

_____

Next Steps: _____

_____

Discussion Topic: _____

Notes: _____

_____

_____

_____

_____

Next Steps: _____

_____

Other things to remember from our time together: _____

_____

_____

If parents will establish a climate conducive to openness, where every person is important and every opinion is valued, they can create a kind of spiritual **SYNERGISM** in the home, where the combined action or cooperation that results is greater than the sum of the individual parts.

Date: _____

Prayer: _____   Record Keeper: _____

In Attendance: _____

_____

Discussion Topic: _____

Notes: _____

_____

_____

_____

_____

Next Steps: _____

_____

Discussion Topic: _____

Notes: _____

_____

_____

_____

_____

Next Steps: _____

_____

Other things to remember from our time together: _____

_____

_____

Date: _____

Prayer: _____ Record Keeper: _____

In Attendance: _____

_____

Discussion Topic: _____

Notes: _____

_____

_____

_____

_____

Next Steps: _____

_____

Discussion Topic: _____

Notes: _____

_____

_____

_____

_____

Next Steps: _____

_____

Other things to remember from our time together: _____

_____

_____

Date: _____

Prayer: _____   Record Keeper: _____

In Attendance: _____

_____

Discussion Topic: _____

Notes: _____

_____

_____

_____

_____

Next Steps: _____

_____

Discussion Topic: _____

Notes: _____

_____

_____

_____

_____

Next Steps: _____

_____

Other things to remember from our time together: _____

_____

_____

Date: _____

Prayer: _____ Record Keeper: _____

In Attendance: _____

_____

Discussion Topic: _____

Notes: _____

_____

_____

_____

_____

Next Steps: _____

_____

Discussion Topic: _____

Notes: _____

_____

_____

_____

_____

Next Steps: _____

_____

Other things to remember from our time together: _____

_____

_____

Date: _____

Prayer: _____ Record Keeper: _____

In Attendance: _____

_____

Discussion Topic: _____

Notes: _____

_____

_____

_____

_____

Next Steps: _____

_____

Discussion Topic: _____

Notes: _____

_____

_____

_____

_____

Next Steps: _____

_____

Other things to remember from our time together: _____

_____

_____

Date: _____

Prayer: _____ Record Keeper: _____

In Attendance: _____

_____

Discussion Topic: _____

Notes: _____

_____

_____

_____

_____

Next Steps: _____

_____

Discussion Topic: _____

Notes: _____

_____

_____

_____

_____

_____

Next Steps: _____

_____

Other things to remember from our time together: _____

_____

_____

Talking about the **COURSE** of **ACTION** makes all the difference.

Date: _____

Prayer: _____ Record Keeper: _____

In Attendance: _____

_____

Discussion Topic: _____

Notes: _____

_____

_____

_____

_____

Next Steps: _____

_____

Discussion Topic: _____

Notes: _____

_____

_____

_____

_____

Next Steps: _____

_____

Other things to remember from our time together: _____

_____

_____

Date: _____

Prayer: _____ Record Keeper: _____

In Attendance: _____

_____

Discussion Topic: _____

Notes: _____

_____

_____

_____

_____

Next Steps: _____

_____

Discussion Topic: _____

Notes: _____

_____

_____

_____

_____

Next Steps: _____

_____

Other things to remember from our time together: _____

_____

_____

Date: _____

Prayer: _____ Record Keeper: _____

In Attendance: _____

_____

Discussion Topic: _____

Notes: _____

_____

_____

_____

_____

Next Steps: _____

_____

Discussion Topic: _____

Notes: _____

_____

_____

_____

_____

Next Steps: _____

_____

Other things to remember from our time together: _____

_____

_____

Date: _____

Prayer: _____   Record Keeper: _____

In Attendance: _____

_____

Discussion Topic: _____

Notes: _____

_____

_____

_____

_____

Next Steps: _____

_____

Discussion Topic: _____

Notes: _____

_____

_____

_____

_____

Next Steps: _____

_____

Other things to remember from our time together: _____

_____

_____

Date: _____

Prayer: _____   Record Keeper: _____

In Attendance: _____

_____

Discussion Topic: _____

Notes: _____

_____

_____

_____

_____

Next Steps: _____

_____

Discussion Topic: _____

Notes: _____

_____

_____

_____

_____

Next Steps: _____

_____

Other things to remember from our time together: _____

_____

_____

Date: _____

Prayer: _____ Record Keeper: _____

In Attendance: _____

_____

Discussion Topic: _____

Notes: _____

_____

_____

_____

_____

Next Steps: _____

_____

Discussion Topic: _____

Notes: _____

_____

_____

_____

_____

Next Steps: _____

_____

Other things to remember from our time together: _____

_____

_____

FAMILY COUNCILS

can be held in one-on-one talks between a parent and a child or among parents and several children. When a husband and wife talk to each other, they are holding a family council.

Date: _____

Prayer: _____   Record Keeper: _____

In Attendance: _____
_____

Discussion Topic: _____

Notes: _____
_____
_____
_____
_____

Next Steps: _____
_____

Discussion Topic: _____

Notes: _____
_____
_____
_____
_____

Next Steps: _____
_____

Other things to remember from our time together: _____
_____
_____

Date: _____

Prayer: _____ Record Keeper: _____

In Attendance: _____

_____

Discussion Topic: _____

Notes: _____

_____

_____

_____

_____

Next Steps: _____

_____

Discussion Topic: _____

Notes: _____

_____

_____

_____

_____

_____

Next Steps: _____

_____

Other things to remember from our time together: _____

_____

_____

Date: _____

Prayer: _____ Record Keeper: _____

In Attendance: _____

_____

Discussion Topic: _____

Notes: _____

_____

_____

_____

_____

Next Steps: _____

_____

Discussion Topic: _____

Notes: _____

_____

_____

_____

_____

Next Steps: _____

_____

Other things to remember from our time together: _____

_____

_____

Date: _____

Prayer: _____ Record Keeper: _____

In Attendance: _____
_____

Discussion Topic: _____

Notes: _____
_____
_____
_____
_____

Next Steps: _____
_____

Discussion Topic: _____

Notes: _____
_____
_____
_____
_____

Next Steps: _____
_____

Other things to remember from our time together: _____
_____
_____

A family council, when conducted with love and with Christlike attributes, will counter the impact of modern technology that often distracts us from spending **QUALITY TIME** with each other and also tends to bring evil right into our homes.

Date: _____

Prayer: _____ Record Keeper: _____

In Attendance: _____

_____

Discussion Topic: _____

Notes: _____

_____

_____

_____

_____

Next Steps: _____

_____

Discussion Topic: _____

Notes: _____

_____

_____

_____

_____

Next Steps: _____

_____

Other things to remember from our time together: _____

_____

_____

Date: _____

Prayer: _____ Record Keeper: _____

In Attendance: _____
_____

Discussion Topic: _____

Notes: _____
_____
_____
_____
_____

Next Steps: _____
_____

Discussion Topic: _____

Notes: _____
_____
_____
_____
_____

Next Steps: _____
_____

Other things to remember from our time together: _____
_____
_____

Date: _____

Prayer: _____ Record Keeper: _____

In Attendance: _____

_____

Discussion Topic: _____

Notes: _____

_____

_____

_____

_____

Next Steps: _____

_____

Discussion Topic: _____

Notes: _____

_____

_____

_____

_____

Next Steps: _____

_____

Other things to remember from our time together: _____

_____

_____

Date: _____

Prayer: _____   Record Keeper: _____

In Attendance: _____

_____

Discussion Topic: _____

Notes: _____

_____

_____

_____

_____

Next Steps: _____

_____

Discussion Topic: _____

Notes: _____

_____

_____

_____

_____

Next Steps: _____

_____

Other things to remember from our time together: _____

_____

_____

Date: _____

Prayer: _____ Record Keeper: _____

In Attendance: _____
_____

Discussion Topic: _____

Notes: _____
_____
_____
_____
_____

Next Steps: _____
_____

Discussion Topic: _____

Notes: _____
_____
_____
_____
_____

Next Steps: _____
_____

Other things to remember from our time together: _____
_____
_____

Date: _____

Prayer: _____   Record Keeper: _____

In Attendance: _____

_____

Discussion Topic: _____

Notes: _____

_____

_____

_____

_____

Next Steps: _____

_____

Discussion Topic: _____

Notes: _____

_____

_____

_____

_____

Next Steps: _____

_____

Other things to remember from our time together: _____

_____

_____

It rests upon each
one of us as mothers
and fathers to do all
we can to prepare
our youth to be
FAITHFUL, righteous
men and women.

Date: _____

Prayer: _____   Record Keeper: _____

In Attendance: _____

_____

Discussion Topic: _____

Notes: _____

_____

_____

_____

_____

Next Steps: _____

_____

Discussion Topic: _____

Notes: _____

_____

_____

_____

_____

Next Steps: _____

_____

Other things to remember from our time together: _____

_____

_____

Date: _____

Prayer: _____   Record Keeper: _____

In Attendance: _____

_____

Discussion Topic: _____

Notes: _____

_____

_____

_____

_____

Next Steps: _____

_____

Discussion Topic: _____

Notes: _____

_____

_____

_____

_____

_____

Next Steps: _____

_____

Other things to remember from our time together: _____

_____

_____

Date: _____

Prayer: _____ Record Keeper: _____

In Attendance: _____

_____

Discussion Topic: _____

Notes: _____

_____

_____

_____

_____

Next Steps: _____

_____

Discussion Topic: _____

Notes: _____

_____

_____

_____

_____

Next Steps: _____

_____

Other things to remember from our time together: _____

_____

_____

Date: _____

Prayer: _____ Record Keeper: _____

In Attendance: _____

_____

Discussion Topic: _____

Notes: _____

_____

_____

_____

_____

Next Steps: _____

_____

Discussion Topic: _____

Notes: _____

_____

_____

_____

_____

Next Steps: _____

_____

Other things to remember from our time together: _____

_____

_____

It is in the **HOME**
where we must teach
the gospel by precept
and by example.

Date: _____

Prayer: _____ Record Keeper: _____

In Attendance: _____

_____

Discussion Topic: _____

Notes: _____

_____

_____

_____

_____

Next Steps: _____

_____

Discussion Topic: _____

Notes: _____

_____

_____

_____

_____

Next Steps: _____

_____

Other things to remember from our time together: _____

_____

_____

Date: _____

Prayer: _____   Record Keeper: _____

In Attendance: _____

_____

Discussion Topic: _____

Notes: _____

_____

_____

_____

_____

Next Steps: _____

_____

Discussion Topic: _____

Notes: _____

_____

_____

_____

_____

Next Steps: _____

_____

Other things to remember from our time together: _____

_____

_____

Date: _____

Prayer: _____   Record Keeper: _____

In Attendance: _____
_____

Discussion Topic: _____

Notes: _____
_____
_____
_____
_____

Next Steps: _____
_____

Discussion Topic: _____

Notes: _____
_____
_____
_____
_____

Next Steps: _____
_____

Other things to remember from our time together: _____
_____
_____

Date: _____

Prayer: _____   Record Keeper: _____

In Attendance: _____
_____

Discussion Topic: _____

Notes: _____
_____
_____
_____
_____

Next Steps: _____
_____

Discussion Topic: _____

Notes: _____
_____
_____
_____
_____

Next Steps: _____
_____

Other things to remember from our time together: _____
_____
_____

Date: _____

Prayer: _____ Record Keeper: _____

In Attendance: _____

_____

Discussion Topic: _____

Notes: _____

_____

_____

_____

_____

Next Steps: _____

_____

Discussion Topic: _____

Notes: _____

_____

_____

_____

_____

Next Steps: _____

_____

Other things to remember from our time together: _____

_____

_____

Date: _____

Prayer: _____   Record Keeper: _____

In Attendance: _____
_____

Discussion Topic: _____

Notes: _____
_____
_____
_____
_____

Next Steps: _____
_____

Discussion Topic: _____

Notes: _____
_____
_____
_____
_____

Next Steps: _____
_____

Other things to remember from our time together: _____
_____
_____

MAY GOD BLESS US

to teach, nurture, and prepare one another within the walls of our homes for the great work that must be done by all of us now and in the future.

Date: _____

Prayer: _____ Record Keeper: _____

In Attendance: _____

_____

Discussion Topic: _____

Notes: _____

_____

_____

_____

_____

Next Steps: _____

_____

Discussion Topic: _____

Notes: _____

_____

_____

_____

_____

Next Steps: _____

_____

Other things to remember from our time together: _____

_____

_____

Date: _____

Prayer: _____ Record Keeper: _____

In Attendance: _____

_____

Discussion Topic: _____

Notes: _____

_____

_____

_____

_____

Next Steps: _____

_____

Discussion Topic: _____

Notes: _____

_____

_____

_____

_____

Next Steps: _____

_____

Other things to remember from our time together: _____

_____

_____

Date: _____

Prayer: _____ Record Keeper: _____

In Attendance: _____

_____

Discussion Topic: _____

Notes: _____

_____

_____

_____

_____

Next Steps: _____

_____

Discussion Topic: _____

Notes: _____

_____

_____

_____

_____

Next Steps: _____

_____

Other things to remember from our time together: _____

_____

_____

Date: _____

Prayer: _____   Record Keeper: _____

In Attendance: _____

_____

Discussion Topic: _____

Notes: _____

_____

_____

_____

_____

Next Steps: _____

_____

Discussion Topic: _____

Notes: _____

_____

_____

_____

_____

Next Steps: _____

_____

Other things to remember from our time together: _____

_____

_____

Nothing shows respect for another person as much as asking for his or her **ADVICE**, because what you are really saying when you ask for advice is, "I appreciate what you know and the experiences you have had, and I value your ideas and suggestions."

Date: _____

Prayer: _____ Record Keeper: _____

In Attendance: _____
_____

Discussion Topic: _____

Notes: _____
_____
_____
_____
_____

Next Steps: _____
_____

Discussion Topic: _____

Notes: _____
_____
_____
_____
_____

Next Steps: _____
_____

Other things to remember from our time together: _____
_____
_____

Date: _____

Prayer: _____ Record Keeper: _____

In Attendance: _____
_____

Discussion Topic: _____
Notes: _____
_____
_____
_____
_____

Next Steps: _____
_____

Discussion Topic: _____
Notes: _____
_____
_____
_____
_____

Next Steps: _____
_____

Other things to remember from our time together: _____
_____
_____

Date: _____

Prayer: _____ Record Keeper: _____

In Attendance: _____

_____

Discussion Topic: _____

Notes: _____

_____

_____

_____

_____

Next Steps: _____

_____

Discussion Topic: _____

Notes: _____

_____

_____

_____

_____

Next Steps: _____

_____

Other things to remember from our time together: _____

_____

_____

Date: _____

Prayer: _____   Record Keeper: _____

In Attendance: _____

_____

Discussion Topic: _____

Notes: _____

_____

_____

_____

_____

Next Steps: _____

_____

Discussion Topic: _____

Notes: _____

_____

_____

_____

_____

Next Steps: _____

_____

Other things to remember from our time together: _____

_____

_____

Date: _____

Prayer: _____   Record Keeper: _____

In Attendance: _____

_____

Discussion Topic: _____

Notes: _____

_____

_____

_____

_____

Next Steps: _____

_____

Discussion Topic: _____

Notes: _____

_____

_____

_____

_____

_____

Next Steps: _____

_____

Other things to remember from our time together: _____

_____

_____

Date: _____

Prayer: _____ Record Keeper: _____

In Attendance: _____

_____

Discussion Topic: _____

Notes: _____

_____

_____

_____

_____

_____

Next Steps: _____

_____

Discussion Topic: _____

Notes: _____

_____

_____

_____

_____

_____

Next Steps: _____

_____

Other things to remember from our time together: _____

_____

_____

EVERY FATHER

needs at least one focused, quality conversation with his sons every month, during which they talk about specific things such as school, friends, feelings, video games, text messaging, worthiness, faith, and testimony.

Date: _____

Prayer: _____   Record Keeper: _____

In Attendance: _____

_____

Discussion Topic: _____

Notes: _____

_____

_____

_____

_____

Next Steps: _____

_____

Discussion Topic: _____

Notes: _____

_____

_____

_____

_____

Next Steps: _____

_____

Other things to remember from our time together: _____

_____

_____

Date: _____

Prayer: _____   Record Keeper: _____

In Attendance: _____
_____

Discussion Topic: _____

Notes: _____
_____
_____
_____
_____

Next Steps: _____
_____

Discussion Topic: _____

Notes: _____
_____
_____
_____
_____

Next Steps: _____
_____

Other things to remember from our time together: _____
_____
_____

Date: _____

Prayer: _____ Record Keeper: _____

In Attendance: _____

_____

Discussion Topic: _____

Notes: _____

_____

_____

_____

_____

Next Steps: _____

_____

Discussion Topic: _____

Notes: _____

_____

_____

_____

_____

Next Steps: _____

_____

Other things to remember from our time together: _____

_____

_____

Date: _____

Prayer: _____ Record Keeper: _____

In Attendance: _____

_____

Discussion Topic: _____

Notes: _____

_____

_____

_____

_____

Next Steps: _____

_____

Discussion Topic: _____

Notes: _____

_____

_____

_____

_____

Next Steps: _____

_____

Other things to remember from our time together: _____

_____

_____

Date: _____

Prayer: _____ Record Keeper: _____

In Attendance: _____

_____

Discussion Topic: _____

Notes: _____

_____

_____

_____

_____

Next Steps: _____

_____

Discussion Topic: _____

Notes: _____

_____

_____

_____

_____

Next Steps: _____

_____

Other things to remember from our time together: _____

_____

_____

Date: _____

Prayer: _____ Record Keeper: _____

In Attendance: _____

_____

Discussion Topic: _____

Notes: _____

_____

_____

_____

_____

Next Steps: _____

_____

Discussion Topic: _____

Notes: _____

_____

_____

_____

_____

Next Steps: _____

_____

Other things to remember from our time together: _____

_____

_____

REMEMBER,

a conversation where you do 90% of the talking is not a conversation.

Date: _____

Prayer: _____ Record Keeper: _____

In Attendance: _____
_____

Discussion Topic: _____

Notes: _____
_____
_____
_____
_____

Next Steps: _____
_____

Discussion Topic: _____

Notes: _____
_____
_____
_____
_____

Next Steps: _____
_____

Other things to remember from our time together: _____
_____
_____

Date: _____

Prayer: _____   Record Keeper: _____

In Attendance: _____

_____

Discussion Topic: _____

Notes: _____

_____

_____

_____

_____

Next Steps: _____

_____

Discussion Topic: _____

Notes: _____

_____

_____

_____

_____

Next Steps: _____

_____

Other things to remember from our time together: _____

_____

_____

Date: _____

Prayer: _____ Record Keeper: _____

In Attendance: _____
_____

Discussion Topic: _____
Notes: _____
_____
_____
_____
_____

Next Steps: _____
_____

Discussion Topic: _____
Notes: _____
_____
_____
_____
_____

Next Steps: _____
_____

Other things to remember from our time together: _____
_____
_____

Date: _____

Prayer: _____   Record Keeper: _____

In Attendance: _____
_____

Discussion Topic: _____

Notes: _____
_____
_____
_____
_____

Next Steps: _____
_____

Discussion Topic: _____

Notes: _____
_____
_____
_____
_____

Next Steps: _____
_____

Other things to remember from our time together: _____
_____
_____

Date: _____

Prayer: _____   Record Keeper: _____

In Attendance: _____

_____

Discussion Topic: _____

Notes: _____

_____

_____

_____

_____

Next Steps: _____

_____

Discussion Topic: _____

Notes: _____

_____

_____

_____

_____

Next Steps: _____

_____

Other things to remember from our time together: _____

_____

_____

Date: _____

Prayer: _____   Record Keeper: _____

In Attendance: _____

_____

Discussion Topic: _____

Notes: _____

_____

_____

_____

_____

Next Steps: _____

_____

Discussion Topic: _____

Notes: _____

_____

_____

_____

_____

Next Steps: _____

_____

Other things to remember from our time together: _____

_____

_____

In the routine of life, we often take our families—our parents and children and siblings—for granted. But in times of danger and need and change, there is no question that what we care about most is our FAMILIES!

Date: _____

Prayer: _____ Record Keeper: _____

In Attendance: _____

_____

Discussion Topic: _____

Notes: _____

_____

_____

_____

_____

Next Steps: _____

_____

Discussion Topic: _____

Notes: _____

_____

_____

_____

_____

Next Steps: _____

_____

Other things to remember from our time together: _____

_____

_____

Date: _____

Prayer: _____ Record Keeper: _____

In Attendance: _____

_____

Discussion Topic: _____

Notes: _____

_____

_____

_____

_____

Next Steps: _____

_____

Discussion Topic: _____

Notes: _____

_____

_____

_____

_____

Next Steps: _____

_____

Other things to remember from our time together: _____

_____

_____

Date: _____

Prayer: _____ Record Keeper: _____

In Attendance: _____

_____

Discussion Topic: _____

Notes: _____

_____

_____

_____

_____

Next Steps: _____

_____

Discussion Topic: _____

Notes: _____

_____

_____

_____

_____

Next Steps: _____

_____

Other things to remember from our time together: _____

_____

_____

Date: _____

Prayer: _____ Record Keeper: _____

In Attendance: _____

_____

Discussion Topic: _____

Notes: _____

_____

_____

_____

_____

Next Steps: _____

_____

Discussion Topic: _____

Notes: _____

_____

_____

_____

_____

Next Steps: _____

_____

Other things to remember from our time together: _____

_____

_____

Nothing is more critically connected to **HAPPINESS**—both our own and that of our children—than how well we love and support one another within the family.

Date: _____

Prayer: _____ Record Keeper: _____

In Attendance: _____
_____

Discussion Topic: _____

Notes: _____
_____
_____
_____
_____
_____

Next Steps: _____
_____

Discussion Topic: _____

Notes: _____
_____
_____
_____
_____
_____

Next Steps: _____
_____

Other things to remember from our time together: _____
_____
_____

Date: _____

Prayer: _____ Record Keeper: _____

In Attendance: _____

_____

Discussion Topic: _____

Notes: _____

_____

_____

_____

_____

Next Steps: _____

_____

Discussion Topic: _____

Notes: _____

_____

_____

_____

_____

Next Steps: _____

_____

Other things to remember from our time together: _____

_____

_____

Date: _____

Prayer: _____ Record Keeper: _____

In Attendance: _____

_____

Discussion Topic: _____

Notes: _____

_____

_____

_____

_____

Next Steps: _____

_____

Discussion Topic: _____

Notes: _____

_____

_____

_____

_____

Next Steps: _____

_____

Other things to remember from our time together: _____

_____

_____

Date: _____

Prayer: _____ Record Keeper: _____

In Attendance: _____

_____

Discussion Topic: _____

Notes: _____

_____

_____

_____

_____

Next Steps: _____

_____

Discussion Topic: _____

Notes: _____

_____

_____

_____

_____

Next Steps: _____

_____

Other things to remember from our time together: _____

_____

_____

Date: _____

Prayer: _____ Record Keeper: _____

In Attendance: _____

_____

Discussion Topic: _____

Notes: _____

_____

_____

_____

_____

Next Steps: _____

_____

Discussion Topic: _____

Notes: _____

_____

_____

_____

_____

Next Steps: _____

_____

Other things to remember from our time together: _____

_____

_____

Date: _____

Prayer: _____ Record Keeper: _____

In Attendance: _____

_____

Discussion Topic: _____

Notes: _____

_____

_____

_____

_____

Next Steps: _____

_____

Discussion Topic: _____

Notes: _____

_____

_____

_____

_____

Next Steps: _____

_____

Other things to remember from our time together: _____

_____

_____

The Church is the kingdom of God on earth, but in the kingdom of heaven, **FAMILIES** will be both the source of our eternal progress and joy and the order of our Heavenly Father.

Date: _____

Prayer: _____   Record Keeper: _____

In Attendance: _____
_____

Discussion Topic: _____

Notes: _____
_____
_____
_____
_____

Next Steps: _____
_____

Discussion Topic: _____

Notes: _____
_____
_____
_____
_____

Next Steps: _____
_____

Other things to remember from our time together: _____
_____
_____

Date: _____

Prayer: _____   Record Keeper: _____

In Attendance: _____

_____

Discussion Topic: _____

Notes: _____

_____

_____

_____

_____

Next Steps: _____

_____

Discussion Topic: _____

Notes: _____

_____

_____

_____

_____

Next Steps: _____

_____

Other things to remember from our time together: _____

_____

_____

Date: _____

Prayer: _____   Record Keeper: _____

In Attendance: _____

_____

Discussion Topic: _____

Notes: _____

_____

_____

_____

_____

_____

Next Steps: _____

_____

Discussion Topic: _____

Notes: _____

_____

_____

_____

_____

Next Steps: _____

_____

Other things to remember from our time together: _____

_____

_____

Date: _____

Prayer: _____ Record Keeper: _____

In Attendance: _____

_____

Discussion Topic: _____

Notes: _____

_____

_____

_____

_____

Next Steps: _____

_____

Discussion Topic: _____

Notes: _____

_____

_____

_____

_____

Next Steps: _____

_____

Other things to remember from our time together: _____

_____

_____

Date: _____

Prayer: _____ Record Keeper: _____

In Attendance: _____
_____

Discussion Topic: _____

Notes: _____
_____
_____
_____
_____

Next Steps: _____
_____

Discussion Topic: _____

Notes: _____
_____
_____
_____
_____

Next Steps: _____
_____

Other things to remember from our time together: _____
_____
_____

Date: _____

Prayer: _____ Record Keeper: _____

In Attendance: _____
_____

Discussion Topic: _____

Notes: _____
_____
_____
_____
_____

Next Steps: _____
_____

Discussion Topic: _____

Notes: _____
_____
_____
_____
_____

Next Steps: _____
_____

Other things to remember from our time together: _____
_____
_____

A family council that is patterned after the councils in heaven, filled with Christlike love, and guided by the Lord's Spirit will help us to **PROTECT OUR FAMILY** from distractions that can steal our precious time together and protect us from the evils of the world.

Date: _____

Prayer: _____ Record Keeper: _____

In Attendance: _____
_____

Discussion Topic: _____

Notes: _____
_____
_____
_____
_____

Next Steps: _____
_____

Discussion Topic: _____

Notes: _____
_____
_____
_____
_____

Next Steps: _____
_____

Other things to remember from our time together: _____
_____
_____

Date: _____

Prayer: _____ Record Keeper: _____

In Attendance: _____

_____

Discussion Topic: _____

Notes: _____

_____

_____

_____

_____

Next Steps: _____

_____

Discussion Topic: _____

Notes: _____

_____

_____

_____

_____

Next Steps: _____

_____

Other things to remember from our time together: _____

_____

_____

Date: _____

Prayer: _____   Record Keeper: _____

In Attendance: _____

_____

Discussion Topic: _____

Notes: _____

_____

_____

_____

_____

Next Steps: _____

_____

Discussion Topic: _____

Notes: _____

_____

_____

_____

_____

Next Steps: _____

_____

Other things to remember from our time together: _____

_____

_____

Date: _____

Prayer: _____   Record Keeper: _____

In Attendance: _____

_____

Discussion Topic: _____

Notes: _____

_____

_____

_____

_____

Next Steps: _____

_____

Discussion Topic: _____

Notes: _____

_____

_____

_____

_____

Next Steps: _____

_____

Other things to remember from our time together: _____

_____

_____

Date: _____

Prayer: _____   Record Keeper: _____

In Attendance: _____

_____

Discussion Topic: _____

Notes: _____

_____

_____

_____

_____

Next Steps: _____

_____

Discussion Topic: _____

Notes: _____

_____

_____

_____

_____

Next Steps: _____

_____

Other things to remember from our time together: _____

_____

_____

Date: _____

Prayer: _____   Record Keeper: _____

In Attendance: _____

_____

Discussion Topic: _____

Notes: _____

_____

_____

_____

_____

Next Steps: _____

_____

Discussion Topic: _____

Notes: _____

_____

_____

_____

_____

Next Steps: _____

_____

Other things to remember from our time together: _____

_____

_____

Our communities and neighborhoods will be safer and stronger as people of all faiths work together to STRENGTHEN FAMILIES.

Date: _____

Prayer: _____ Record Keeper: _____

In Attendance: _____

_____

Discussion Topic: _____

Notes: _____

_____

_____

_____

_____

Next Steps: _____

_____

Discussion Topic: _____

Notes: _____

_____

_____

_____

_____

Next Steps: _____

_____

Other things to remember from our time together: _____

_____

_____

Date: _____

Prayer: _____ Record Keeper: _____

In Attendance: _____

_____

Discussion Topic: _____

Notes: _____

_____

_____

_____

_____

Next Steps: _____

_____

Discussion Topic: _____

Notes: _____

_____

_____

_____

_____

Next Steps: _____

_____

Other things to remember from our time together: _____

_____

_____

Date: _____

Prayer: _____   Record Keeper: _____

In Attendance: _____

_____

Discussion Topic: _____

Notes: _____

_____

_____

_____

_____

Next Steps: _____

_____

Discussion Topic: _____

Notes: _____

_____

_____

_____

_____

Next Steps: _____

_____

Other things to remember from our time together: _____

_____

_____

Date: _____

Prayer: _____ Record Keeper: _____

In Attendance: _____

_____

Discussion Topic: _____

Notes: _____

_____

_____

_____

_____

Next Steps: _____

_____

Discussion Topic: _____

Notes: _____

_____

_____

_____

_____

Next Steps: _____

_____

Other things to remember from our time together: _____

_____

_____

No matter who or
what we are, we help
ourselves when we help

FAMILIES.

Date: _____

Prayer: _____ Record Keeper: _____

In Attendance: _____

_____

Discussion Topic: _____

Notes: _____

_____

_____

_____

_____

Next Steps: _____

_____

Discussion Topic: _____

Notes: _____

_____

_____

_____

_____

Next Steps: _____

_____

Other things to remember from our time together: _____

_____

_____

Date: _____

Prayer: _____ Record Keeper: _____

In Attendance: _____

_____

Discussion Topic: _____

Notes: _____

_____

_____

_____

_____

_____

Next Steps: _____

_____

Discussion Topic: _____

Notes: _____

_____

_____

_____

_____

_____

Next Steps: _____

_____

Other things to remember from our time together: _____

_____

_____

Date: _____

Prayer: _____ Record Keeper: _____

In Attendance: _____

_____

Discussion Topic: _____

Notes: _____

_____

_____

_____

_____

Next Steps: _____

_____

Discussion Topic: _____

Notes: _____

_____

_____

_____

_____

Next Steps: _____

_____

Other things to remember from our time together: _____

_____

_____

Date: _____

Prayer: _____   Record Keeper: _____

In Attendance: _____

_____

Discussion Topic: _____

Notes: _____

_____

_____

_____

_____

Next Steps: _____

_____

Discussion Topic: _____

Notes: _____

_____

_____

_____

_____

Next Steps: _____

_____

Other things to remember from our time together: _____

_____

_____

Date: _____

Prayer: _____ Record Keeper: _____

In Attendance: _____

_____

Discussion Topic: _____

Notes: _____

_____

_____

_____

_____

Next Steps: _____

_____

Discussion Topic: _____

Notes: _____

_____

_____

_____

_____

Next Steps: _____

_____

Other things to remember from our time together: _____

_____

_____

Date: _____

Prayer: _____ Record Keeper: _____

In Attendance: _____

_____

Discussion Topic: _____

Notes: _____

_____

_____

_____

_____

Next Steps: _____

_____

Discussion Topic: _____

Notes: _____

_____

_____

_____

_____

Next Steps: _____

_____

Other things to remember from our time together: _____

_____

_____

As your leaders, we call
upon members of the
Church everywhere to put
FAMILY FIRST
and to identify specific
ways to strengthen their
individual families.

Date: _____

Prayer: _____ Record Keeper: _____

In Attendance: _____

_____

Discussion Topic: _____

Notes: _____

_____

_____

_____

_____

Next Steps: _____

_____

Discussion Topic: _____

Notes: _____

_____

_____

_____

_____

Next Steps: _____

_____

Other things to remember from our time together: _____

_____

_____

Date: _____

Prayer: _____ Record Keeper: _____

In Attendance: _____
_____

Discussion Topic: _____

Notes: _____
_____
_____
_____
_____

Next Steps: _____
_____

Discussion Topic: _____

Notes: _____
_____
_____
_____
_____

Next Steps: _____
_____

Other things to remember from our time together: _____
_____
_____

Date: _____

Prayer: _____   Record Keeper: _____

In Attendance: _____

_____

Discussion Topic: _____

Notes: _____

_____

_____

_____

_____

_____

Next Steps: _____

_____

Discussion Topic: _____

Notes: _____

_____

_____

_____

_____

_____

Next Steps: _____

_____

Other things to remember from our time together: _____

_____

_____

Date: _____

Prayer: _____ Record Keeper: _____

In Attendance: _____

_____

Discussion Topic: _____

Notes: _____

_____

_____

_____

_____

Next Steps: _____

_____

Discussion Topic: _____

Notes: _____

_____

_____

_____

_____

Next Steps: _____

_____

Other things to remember from our time together: _____

_____

_____

Date: _____

Prayer: _____ Record Keeper: _____

In Attendance: _____

_____

Discussion Topic: _____

Notes: _____

_____

_____

_____

_____

_____

Next Steps: _____

_____

Discussion Topic: _____

Notes: _____

_____

_____

_____

_____

_____

Next Steps: _____

_____

Other things to remember from our time together: _____

_____

_____

Date: _____

Prayer: _____   Record Keeper: _____

In Attendance: _____

_____

Discussion Topic: _____

Notes: _____

_____

_____

_____

_____

Next Steps: _____

_____

Discussion Topic: _____

Notes: _____

_____

_____

_____

_____

Next Steps: _____

_____

Other things to remember from our time together: _____

_____

_____

Most of the time,
the best thing you
can do is just
LISTEN.

Date: _____

Prayer: _____   Record Keeper: _____

In Attendance: _____

_____

Discussion Topic: _____

Notes: _____

_____

_____

_____

_____

Next Steps: _____

_____

Discussion Topic: _____

Notes: _____

_____

_____

_____

_____

Next Steps: _____

_____

Other things to remember from our time together: _____

_____

_____

Date: _____

Prayer: _____ Record Keeper: _____

In Attendance: _____

_____

Discussion Topic: _____

Notes: _____

_____

_____

_____

_____

Next Steps: _____

_____

Discussion Topic: _____

Notes: _____

_____

_____

_____

_____

Next Steps: _____

_____

Other things to remember from our time together: _____

_____

_____

Date: _____

Prayer: _____   Record Keeper: _____

In Attendance: _____

_____

Discussion Topic: _____

Notes: _____

_____

_____

_____

_____

Next Steps: _____

_____

Discussion Topic: _____

Notes: _____

_____

_____

_____

_____

Next Steps: _____

_____

Other things to remember from our time together: _____

_____

_____

Date: _____

Prayer: _____   Record Keeper: _____

In Attendance: _____

_____

Discussion Topic: _____

Notes: _____

_____

_____

_____

_____

Next Steps: _____

_____

Discussion Topic: _____

Notes: _____

_____

_____

_____

_____

Next Steps: _____

_____

Other things to remember from our time together: _____

_____

_____

Date: _____

Prayer: _____ Record Keeper: _____

In Attendance: _____
_____

Discussion Topic: _____

Notes: _____
_____
_____
_____
_____

Next Steps: _____
_____

Discussion Topic: _____

Notes: _____
_____
_____
_____
_____

Next Steps: _____
_____

Other things to remember from our time together: _____
_____
_____

Date: _____

Prayer: _____   Record Keeper: _____

In Attendance: _____

_____

Discussion Topic: _____

Notes: _____

_____

_____

_____

_____

Next Steps: _____

_____

Discussion Topic: _____

Notes: _____

_____

_____

_____

_____

Next Steps: _____

_____

Other things to remember from our time together: _____

_____

_____

Let us remember
that the basic council
of the Church is the
FAMILY COUNCIL.

Date: _____

Prayer: _____ Record Keeper: _____

In Attendance: _____

_____

Discussion Topic: _____

Notes: _____

_____

_____

_____

_____

Next Steps: _____

_____

Discussion Topic: _____

Notes: _____

_____

_____

_____

_____

Next Steps: _____

_____

Other things to remember from our time together: _____

_____

_____

Date: _____

Prayer: _____   Record Keeper: _____

In Attendance: _____

_____

Discussion Topic: _____

Notes: _____

_____

_____

_____

_____

Next Steps: _____

_____

Discussion Topic: _____

Notes: _____

_____

_____

_____

_____

Next Steps: _____

_____

Other things to remember from our time together: _____

_____

_____

Date: _____

OTHER NOTES

Date: _____

OTHER NOTES

Date: _____

Date: _____

Date: _____

Date: _____

Date: _____

OTHER NOTES

Date: _____

Date: _____

Date: _____

Date: _____

Date: _____

Date: _____

OTHER NOTES

Date: _____

OTHER NOTES

Date: _____

OTHER NOTES

Date: _____

Date: _____

OTHER NOTES

Date: _____

Date: _____

OTHER NOTES

Date: _____

Date: _____